WIGMEN
OF PAPUA

WIGMEN OF PAPUA

James Sinclair

The Jacaranda Press

First published 1973 by
JACARANDA PRESS PTY. LTD.
46 Douglas Street, Milton, Q.
32 Church Street, Ryde, N.S.W.
37 Little Bourke Street, Melbourne, Vic.
142 Colin Street, West Perth, W.A.
154 Marion Road, West Richmond, S.A.
57 France Street, Auckland, N.Z.
P.O. Box 3395, Port Moresby, P.N.G.
122 Regents Park Road, London NW1
70A Greenleaf Road, Singapore 10
P.O. Box 239, Makati, Rizal, Philippines

Typesetting by Savage & Co.
Printed in Hong Kong

© J. Sinclair 1973

National Library of Australia
Card Number and ISBN 0 7016 0577 4

BY THE SAME AUTHOR
Behind the Ranges, Melbourne University Press, Melbourne, 1966
The Outside Man, Lansdowne Press, Melbourne, 1969
Sepik Pilot, Lansdowne Press, Melbourne, 1971
The Highlanders, Jacaranda Press, Brisbane, 1971

Contents

Acknowledgments

This is not an anthropological treatise. I have, however, been assisted greatly by the published work of R. M. Glasse on the Huri, and by correspondence with Charles Modjeska in relation to the Duna. I am sure that neither of these anthropologists would agree with everything that I have written, and I am alone responsible for what appears in this book.

I would also like to acknowledge the assistance given to me by John S. Hicks, Assistant District Commissioner, Koroba.

Dedication

To my friend, Andrew Andagari Wabiria, Member of the Second House of Assembly for the Koroba Open Electorate and Assistant Ministerial Member for Lands, Surveys and Mines . . .
and, as a very small boy, an interpreter and general assistant with our patrols

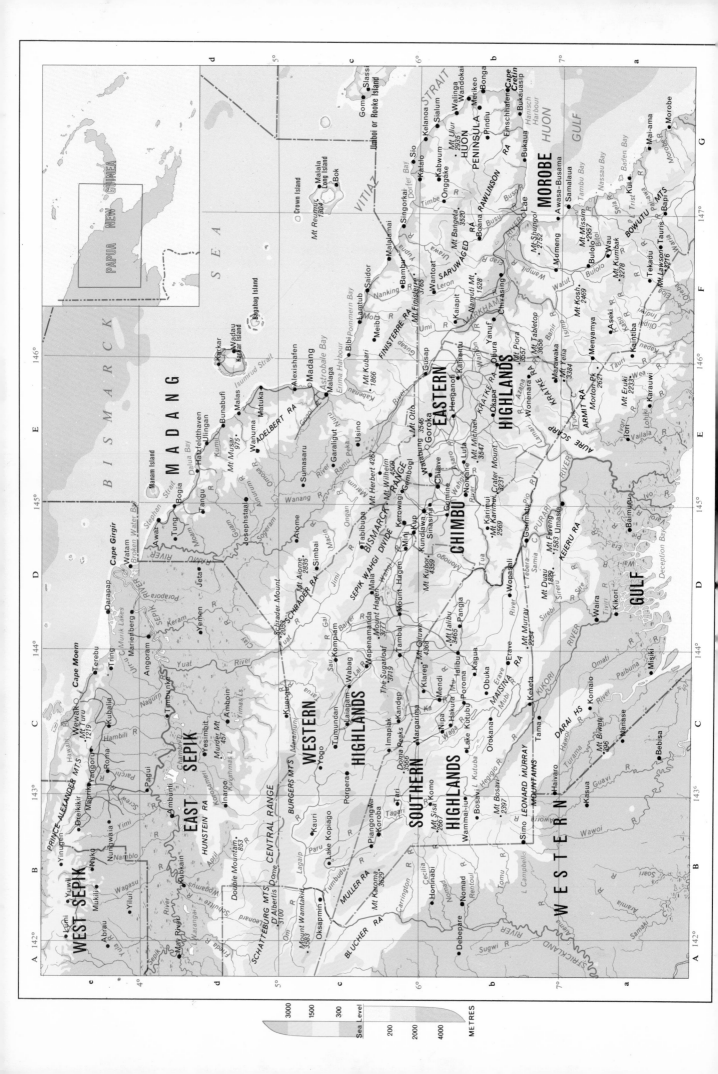

Author's Note

The photographs that illustrate this book were taken during the years 1955 to 1958 in the Southern Highlands of Papua, mainly in the sub-districts of Tari and Koroba, and in the Western Highlands of New Guinea. Koroba patrols operated extensively across the former territorial border. Readers will note that the majority of the photographs are of men: women and children seldom appear. There is a good reason for this. The pictures were taken by myself, as a patrol officer leading a long series of exploratory and pacification patrols into country then classed as "restricted," closed to all unauthorized entry. Many of the people contacted by our patrols had had limited experience of the Government; often we encountered people who had not been previously contacted. It is understandable then, that the men would seek to keep their women and children away from us as much as possible.

In this book I have attempted to present a picture of the Huri and Duna wigmen as they were at the time of early contact by the patrols. Such patrols were organized by what is today known as the Division of District Administration of the Department of the Administrator. This has been known at various times as the Department of the Government Secretary, as District Services and Native Affairs, as Native Affairs and as District Administration. It is, unfortunately, becoming customary today in Papua New Guinea for the work of the "kiaps," or patrol officers to be slighted and even vilified. Generally this is done by academics of little practical experience of New Guinea and by the emerging generation of students whose mentors the kiaps were. Perhaps this is inevitable, for Papua New Guinea is fast growing up and soon will join the international community of independent nations, and naturally the young Papuan or New Guinean tends to resent the recent colonial past. But when the full history of this country comes to be written, the work of the kiaps will be seen in perspective as being an honourable and indispensable work, without which the Papua New Guinea of the future might not have been.

A Note on the Photographs

All of the colour photographs that illustrate this book were made on the old Kodachrome ASA 10 film, which has long since gone out of production, to the lasting regret of many photographers.

The black and white photographs were made on Adox KB 14 and KB 17 film, and on Kodak Panatomic-X. All were developed in Kodak D76, diluted 1 to 1 with water and used as a one-shot developer. The paper developer was Kodak Dektol. Papers used were by Mimosa, Agfa and Ilford.

Camera equipment employed would not be highly regarded today: a Praktica 35 mm single-lens reflex and a very early model Pentacon 35 mm single-lens reflex. The Praktica was equipped with a waist level finder, while the Pentacon had an eye-level prism finder. Focusing screens were plain ground glass. Neither camera featured a built-in exposure meter system, and I employed the rugged and reliable Weston Master II over these years.

Lenses, listed below, were not matched, were manually operated with no automatic features, and were thus slow in operation.

LENSES:
f4.5, 35 mm Enna Lithagon, pre-set
f2, 58 mm Zeiss Biotar, pre-set
f2, 80 mm Schneider Xenon, manual
f2.8, 135 mm Steinheil Quinar, pre-set

1 The Wigmen's Country

I first saw the great Tari Basin of the Huri[1] people in January 1955. Flying in from Mendi, the headquarters of the Southern Highlands district,[2] the aerial route led the old Norseman aircraft through the Gap between the mountains called Ne and Ambua by the Huri, to a height of over 3,000 metres. Pillowy banks of pure white, wind-driven cumulus cloud choked the pass, forcing the pilot to climb. We burst through the cloud and into the vast basin, a glorious sight in the hard morning sun. It was green, blue and brown beneath us: the brown of the countless tiny squares of gardens, the blue of the hazy mountains that ringed the basin, the green of this beautiful land, the home of the race of wig-wearers that we know as the Huri.

1 The anthropologists call them "Huli"; the spelling I have used is that adopted by the Administration.
2 There are four Highlands Districts in Papua New Guinea: the other three are the Chimbu, the Eastern and the Western Districts. Together, they contain some 950,000 of the estimated two and a quarter million population of Papua New Guinea.

The Strickland Gorge at sunset. There is little flat land in this wild, grim country

These sturdy, warlike people, are subsistence farmers, growing their sweet potatoes, taro and sugar cane in the fine fenced gardens that flank their scattered garden hamlets. They have many notable characteristics, perhaps the most striking being the great flower-decked wigs of human hair worn by the adult males, a custom shared by their neighbours and close cultural relatives, the Duna, and by certain groups in the Western Highlands.

There are some 38,000 of the Huri, and the total area of their territory exceeds 2,500 square kilometres. The Duna are less numerous—under 10,000—and they are more sparsely distributed over the deteriorating country further to the north-west, between the sub-district stations of Koroba, and Lake Kapiagu in the Western Highlands, and north again to the grimly magnificent limestone country of the Strickland Gorge.

It is a country isolated by geography and by history. Guarded by the massive bulk of the Muller and Karius Ranges to the south and the Central Range system to the north, this country is in the very centre of the mainland New Guinea. The Southern Highlands was the last of the Highlands districts to be

The Strickland Gorge

explored. The first patrol, in 1935, approaching from the south, took months to break through to the Tari Basin and lost three of its number from sickness and exhaustion. The discoverer of the Huri country called it the "Papuan Wonderland."

Huri men smoking their big bamboo pipes, peer into the camera lens. They wonder what the *hunavie* is up to. The wigs are decorated with the typical Huri maroon and yellow everlastings

2 The People

When the first white men walked through the country of the Huri, they found a culture quite different from any previously known in Papua. They found a relatively dense population of light-skinned, stocky warrior farmers, the men wearing great

3

mushroom-shaped wigs of human hair, decorated with yellow and red everlasting daisies, and blowing endlessly on Pan pipes of bamboo. They found no villages. The wigmen lived in garden settlements, scattered over the open grass. Here and there, amongst the gardens, could be seen the bark coffins of the dead, held up on platforms by pens of bush timber, one to two metres high. Great trenches, up to five metres deep, criss-crossed the floor of the Basin. These huge inter-connected trenches, dug by hand with simple digging-sticks, were a feature of the Huri culture. Men could secretly move along these for considerable distances and they were much used in tribal warfare. They also served to control the movement of pigs and to delineate clan land boundaries. The Duna wigmen, living in more difficult, broken terrain, never developed any similar trench system.

A fine Huri child at his mother's breast

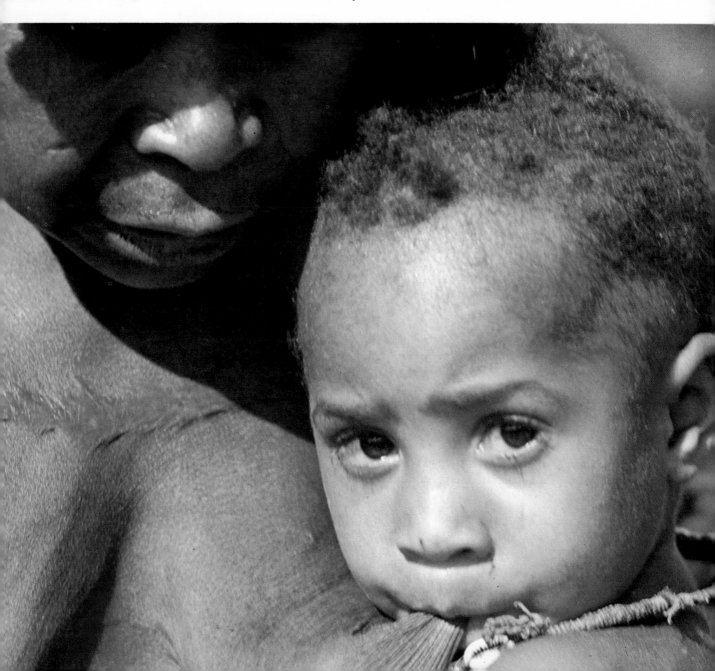

The initial explorers found no steel in this land. The shells that the people wore as ornaments were generally of poor quality: undersized cowrie and **tambu** shell, cracked **komakoma** and small crescents of mother-of-pearl. The isolated country of these wigmen was at the very end of the great traditional trade routes from the coast, and only the least desirable shell found its way through the avaricious hands of the intervening trading communities to the country of the Huri and the Duna.

The first patrol soon found proof of the warlike nature of the wigmen. Attacked by arrow-firing warriors, the officers and police were compelled to use their rifles in self-defence. The wigmen pressed home their attacks with great determination, for warfare was the dominant interest of this society.

A group of Duna men stand silently on a grassy ridge as the patrol passes through their land

Duna of the Tumbuda River watching the passing of the patrol from afar. This reserve was typical of the people of this country during the early contact phase

From the day of his birth, the Huri boy—and to a somewhat lesser extent, the Duna—was taught that his finest destiny was to become a warrior, to defend and extend the interests of his family and his clan by armed force. To achieve this object, clans would commonly enter into temporary alliances with neighbouring groups; the allies of today could well be the enemies of tomorrow. Such temporary alliances were often openly mercenary; there was no chivalry in this warrior society. Pay-back, the savage custom found throughout the Highlands, was also present here. If an injury were done to a clan, then that injury must be repaid, either by property settlement or by retaliation. This custom, of course, produced a history of involved, interlocking feuds. It ensured that at any given time a number of unresolved feuds would keep a given district in a state of armed tension.

Opposite page: Huri fight leaders. The man on the left is Warago, a famous warrior. He wears a fine mother-of-pearl crescent and carries a large bone dagger in his waist girdle of cane

Below: Huri men dancing. The mature man at the right wears the bachelor's wig and finery of his young manhood and he bangs the kundu drum as he leaps and chants. These hand-drums are of hour glass shapes, cut and hollowed from a single piece of wood and with a drum-head of the skin of an iguana, tuned by the application of lumps of tree gum

Below left: Another view of Huri male dancers

A Duna widow. She is in mourning for her husband, killed during a tribal battle. Her face is heavily plastered with yellow clay

Right: An impressive Duna fight leader

A Duna man looks sternly at the camera. He is from the Paru. His wig is covered with coarse woven netting and around his neck he wears a tiny piece of mother-of-pearl —evidence of the poverty of these isolated bush people

The Huri and Duna people did not scorn the use of poison and magic, with appropriate ritual and preparation, to even their scores. In any serious dispute such as unrequited deaths, women, land or pig troubles, open warfare involving pitched battle between opposing armed groups, was usual. Huri wars were fearsome. A major war could involve a thousand or fifteen hundred screaming bowmen, marshalled into squads by recognized fight leaders. Such a war could last for months and result in scores of deaths. The Huri fought to destroy. He showed no mercy to his enemies. Women and children, the sick and the aged were alike slaughtered when caught. He showed no mercy towards the property and lands of his enemies. Whenever he

8

could, he burned houses, killed pigs, slashed down food trees, destroyed gardens. The Huri was an enthusiastic proponent of the scorched-earth policy long before Western nations. Wars in the Duna were invariably on a smaller scale. The smaller, scattered population did not allow the mobilization of Huri-style armies, but the end result was the same: total destruction of the enemy.

Deaths and injuries suffered in wars had to be paid for, if future outbreaks were to be avoided. And here the pig, as prized by these wigmen as by all the peoples of the Highlands, played his vital part in stabilizing social relationships. Among the Huri, it was usual for the opposing sides to exchange a number of sides of slaughtered pigs as a token that hostilities were concluded.

Payments of pig-sides were made for death and injury. As many as a hundred pigs might be required to compensate for the death of a senior warrior, ten to fifteen for a serious arrow wound. So many pigs could be required to settle all payments resulting from a major war that it could be many months before the affair was concluded.

Among the Duna, a poorer people with fewer pigs, it was common in some areas for the fight leader to pay pig-sides to the next of kin of those on his own side killed and injured, rather than compensating the enemy. Payments could therefore be kept within economically reasonable limits, and if necessary more time could be allowed to complete the payments.

Young Duna widow, from the Paru River. Invariably timid, the young women would seldom linger in our camps

A fine old Duna patriarch. He wears tattered wing feathers from the kunai pheasant tucked into his wig, which is draped with opossum fur. His wiry whiskers are grey with age. He has many wives and many children

The bow and arrow was the principal weapon. Arrow heads used in normal warfare were smooth, tapering pencils of blackpalm bound into shafts of **pitpit** cane. The bows, short and heavy, were made of blackpalm with the strings of scraped bamboo. Men invariably carried bone knives, made from the leg bone of the cassowary, and adzes of stone set into angled wooden hafts, but these were more tool than weapon.

Another characteristic of the Huri and Duna common to many other Highlands cultures was their general distrust and suspicion of women. Male-dominated, this society was concerned with maintaining the strength and status of the male. Undue contact with women was considered to be the source of sickness and debility, and this led to separation of men and women, even to the maintenance of separate households. Men would never enter the women's houses and vice versa; marital relations usually took place in the gardens. Menstruating women were considered to be very dangerous. Sexual intercourse with such a woman would be fatal to the male. Even to be sighted by a menstruating woman could lead to premature senility. No man would touch food prepared by such a woman; indeed, men normally prepared and cooked their own food to ensure that it was not woman-contaminated. Young bachelors

Opposite page: A wise old Huri veteran

A shy young Huri girl visits our camp with her companions. In the early months few women visited our camps, except fleetingly

An aged Duna woman. Her hands bear the marks of a lifetime of toil

Right: A young Duna child. His proud father has given him a fine necklet of *girigiri* shells to wear. His young body carries the scars of injury and disease but he is a strong and healthy boy

Above far right: Paru River Duna carrying a fine string of *girigiri* shell strung to a long decorated pole. He is making a ceremonial exchange in connection with the forthcoming marriage of a kinsman

Far right: Duna men sit watching the movements of the patrol, sucking on their bamboo pipes in wary friendliness. Their wigs, typical of the northern Duna, are ragged and they boast very little decoration. The man at left rear is a Huri—note the differences in the wig pattern

made and tilled their own gardens without the assistance of women. Menstrual blood was considered by the Huri to be the most deadly of poisons. Even the normal act of intercourse with one's wife was not to be lightly undertaken.

Generally, the Huri man would not consider marrying any woman to whom he could trace a genealogical connection. Among the Duna, whose larger clan groups were distributed over great areas of country, it was frequently difficult for a man to avoid marrying a woman with whom he had genealogical ties. A brideprice was always paid, usually fifteen pigs plus an assortment of lesser items among the Huri.

Although the Huri and Duna had no village settlements, and lived in homestead groups and family units throughout their garden lands, their society was organized along complex lines. As always in Melanesian societies, land and rights in land were of overriding importance. In an account of this nature, one cannot avoid generalizing, for the subject is tremendously complex. For our purposes it can be assumed that among the Huri and Duna a man had land rights wherever he could trace an ancestor. The typical Huri male had not one, but several households: in the land of his father's clan, his mother's clan, the clan of any known ancestor. Given the relatively dense population distribution of the Huri, the result was a complicated network of rights and obligations, often cut across by

feud and warfare. The Duna, with their different circumstances, seldom maintained more than a single household.

These people had of course, no written language but genealogies could usually be traced for four or five generations back: sometimes considerably further. This was the basic factor regulating land rights.

The Huri boy was removed from the household of his mother to that of his father at a very early age. His progress to full manhood was marked by elaborate ceremonial, culminating in the bachelor's ritual in his late teens. During this period of his life the young Huri was expected to avoid all association with women, particularly sexual association. For eighteen months or so, the young initiates of the age group received instruction and training from well skilled elders, and then were entitled to wear the elaborate, beautifully made red wig of the young bachelor. Their faces carefully painted in identical patterns with red and yellow ochre, their bodies a shiny red with applications of tigaso tree oil, groups of the young bachelors would stalk silently throughout the land, their crescent shaped wigs trimmed with strips of cuscus fur and the iridescent blue breast-shield of the Superb Bird-of-Paradise, and with the plumes of the cassowary—objects of admiration to all. The young bachelors would parade, at regular intervals over a period of twelve months.

The shimmering plumes of the Raggiana bird-of-paradise, very common in the country towards the Strickland

Kunai orchids, found in the grasslands of the Huri and the Duna

The young bachelors. Note the brilliant use of coloured ochres for facial decoration, tiny feathers and the wing plumes of the cassowary. Cassowary plumage was a characteristic item of the formal dress of the warrior in many societies of Papua and of New Guinea

The Tege rites were also of great significance to the young men. These rites, often extending over a period of years, involved the sacrifice of pigs to the deities Ne (regarded by the Huri as the creator), to Korimogolo and others. They culminated in a week-long ceremony called Tege, involving hundreds of participants, climaxing in a spectacular ordeal of fire walking, where young men ran, bare footed, through a lane of red-hot embers while on either side the elders struck at them with switches.

All of this ritual emphasized the superiority of the male over the female, but women had a definite and important place in the society of the Huri and Duna wigmen. The women had the major responsibility for the daily care of the most precious asset of the household, the pig. It is difficult to overstate the importance of the pig to the Huri and Duna people. Greatly desired as food, the pig had a far wider value: all social and political transactions depended upon the pig as a unit of currency. A man's ultimate status in his community depended upon the size of his pig wealth. During the daylight hours, the pigs were grazed on household land and abandoned gardens, but at night they were penned in the women's houses.

Opposite page: A young Huri bachelor proudly parades through the camp. The reddish tinge of the tigaso oil body dressing is very noticeable. There is remarkably little variation in the formal painted facial design worn by the young bachelors during this important stage of their lives

Below left: A Huri baby in his mother's arms. He is not very clean—his hair is matted with filth—but he is a fine strong boy. Perhaps he is today a student at the University of Papua New Guinea?

Below: A young Huri dandy with his Pan pipes. His wig is decked with yellow and maroon everlastings and through his nasal septum he wears a thin stalk of pitpit. The texture of the net bag, so common in the Highlands, is clearly seen

Garden clearing, Huri style. The heavy initial work of clearing the bush of timber and secondary growth is the task of the male. As this picture shows, a considerable amount of work with primitive tools was involved

Young Duna girl awaits her turn to sell food to the patrol. The crescent she wears around her neck is cut from a discarded food tin. Few, if any, girls of her age would have a genuine mother-of-pearl crescent to wear

These people were subsistence gardeners, completely dependent upon what they grew to sustain life: hunting and food gathering in the mountains flanking their country, contributed very little indeed to daily diet. Men and women shared the labour of establishing the garden. They followed the shifting cultivation method common in New Guinea. Men performed the heavy tasks of initial clearing and fencing of the garden, while the women completed the clearing and prepared the ground for planting, which was undertaken by both. The staple food was the sweet potato, of many recognized varieties, but other foods were grown: bananas, taro, sugar cane, beans, yams, greens and relishes. Skilful gardeners, they used primitive tools—the digging stick and the stone adze—to good effect. The sweet potatoes were planted in mounds, enriched with ashes, and the yield in good soils was high; the potatoes matured in three to six months.

18

Duna women were invariably shy upon early contact. They keep well out of harm's way until the patrol is ready to purchase their net bags of food

Magical rites were associated with every stage of the preparation of gardens and the harvesting of the crop: the Huri and Duna believed that malign influences would spoil their crops if the appropriate ghosts and spirits were not propitiated in accordance with tribal custom. Indeed, a belief in ghosts and spirits governed every aspect of their lives. All deaths from natural causes were held to be the result of magical or supernatural influences. There were appropriate rituals and courses of action for every contingency. Not uncommonly, individual Huri would be seized by a strange disorder characterized by uncontrolled body tremors, violent and unpredictable behaviour and mental delusions. Such a state was known as **lulu,** and persons suffering from **lulu** often brought about inter-clan warfare, for a **lulu-man** frequently would destroy gardens and attack and kill innocent passers-by when in the grip of his affliction. Normally, fellow-clansmen would restrain their deranged fellow forcibly, until the attack had passed. Both men and women were subject to the curse of **lulu**, which was held to be caused by supernatural influences. These must then be wooed by the ceremonial slaughter of pigs.

A Huri woman in the grip of the condition known as *"lulu"* prancing and singing in her sweet potato garden

The people believed in the existence of a soul, or life spirit. A sleeper should never be abruptly awakened, lest his soul, wandering from the sleeping body, take flight. There was no equivalent to the Christian's belief in an afterlife, but the ghosts of the departed were believed to influence the affairs of the living. The Duna held that upon death the souls of the dead turned into round black stones, called Auwi, about ten centimetres in diameter. These were venerated and were often found in their territory.

3 The Coming of the White Man

In 1930, the prospectors Michael Leahy and Michael Dwyer[3] made their incredible journey from the Upper Ramu, south to the head-waters of the Purari and down that river system to the Papuan coast. It was a journey of profound significance in the history of the exploration of the Highlands. For until this journey, it was popularly held that the interior of the mainland was a waste of high, impenetrable mountains, inhabited, if at all, by a few nomadic tribes. Leahy and Dwyer proved that the interior was in fact heavily populated. The story of the rapid exploration of the New Guinea Highlands that followed on the 1930 journey has been told many times. Later that year Leahy and Dwyer made a second journey, through to the valleys of the Bena Bena and the Asaro. Then, in 1933, came the famous expedition made jointly by Mick and Dan Leahy and Ken Spinks, on behalf of the Wau gold mining firm of New Guinea Goldfields Ltd, and by James L. Taylor, Assistant District Officer, and his police detachment on behalf of the Mandated Territory Administration. This penetrated for the first time the valleys of the Chimbu and the Wahgi, with their half-million population. In 1934 the Leahys probed to the west of the base camp they had established with Taylor at Mount Hagen. They

3 See Sinclair, J., *The Highlanders*, Jacaranda Press, Brisbane, 1971.

20

went as far as Mt Giluwe and Mt Ialibu, in Papua's Southern Highlands, but they did not travel far into Papua and never came into contact with the Huri and Duna.

The first white men to see these people were almost certainly two tough, quiet prospectors, Tom and Jack Fox. The Fox brothers, identical twins, were born in 1892, in England. They arrived in Australia in time to serve in the A.I.F. during the Great War. Both came to New Guinea in 1922, and early in 1934 to Kainantu, prospecting for gold. Restless men, they moved to the Bena Bena and so to the west, to the Mount Hagen base. In late August 1934, Tom and Jack Fox left Hagen with sixteen carriers for the completely unknown country to the west, looking for gold. They carried bacon and flour; rice for their carriers; a meagre supply of prospecting equipment and camp gear. The Fox brothers were not ones to keep detailed logs of their travels, although they did maintain a brief daily diary. They carried no survey instruments. It is impossible to be certain how far to the west they went, but it seems certain that they reached the headwaters of the great Strickland River. The stories told today in the sparse Duna settlements in the region of Lake Kapiagu support this.[4] We can thus credit Tom and Jack Fox with being the first white men to make contact with a handful of the Duna wigmen.

In the following year, the centuries-long isolation of the Huri was breached.

The spectacular discoveries made in the Highlands of the Mandated Territory of New Guinea threw no light upon the great white space on the map to the south of the territorial border, in Papua. It is unfortunately true that there was limited liaison on such matters between the administrations of both Papua and New Guinea before the war, even though both administrations were staffed by Australians and received their policy directions from the same source, Canberra. Little detailed information was available to the Papuan Administration on the work of the patrols and the prospectors in the newly-opened Highlands. At this point it is obvious that a

4 See Sinclair, J., *The Outside Man*, Lansdowne Press, Melbourne, 1969.

combined approach, a pooling of information, could have made the work of the Papuan patrols, far easier. When the Huri people were discovered, the officers leading the patrol were not aware of the magnitude and the implications of the discoveries on the other side of the border; they did not even know that shell, not steel, was the most valued item of trade in these high grassed valleys. By 1935 this fact had been well and truly established on the New Guinea side.

By 1935 the only considerable block of completely unexplored territory remaining in Papua was the country between the Strickland and the Purari Rivers—today's Southern Highlands. Some limited exploratory work had been done on the fringes; Theodore Bevan ascended the Kikori River for 160 kilometres in 1887, and in 1908 Donald MacKay and his coal prospecting party took three months to travel up the Purari to a point only 128 kilometres from the coast.

In 1910–11 the ill-fated Staniforth Smith expedition made an abortive attempt to cross from the Kikori to the Strickland, losing eleven carriers and achieving very little of value.

H. J. Ryan succeeded in travelling from the Kikori as far west as the Awarra during a notable patrol in 1913, and in 1922 L. A. Flint and H. M. Saunders patrolled to the valley of the Samberigi, the deepest penetration from the coast yet achieved.

The 1929 patrol of B. W. Faithorn and C. Champion up the Turama and to the Erave-Purari junction came the closest to discovering the heavily populated Southern Highlands grasslands. Champion, from a vantage point, saw smoke trails and pale open grass away to the north, but the patrol kept on to the Papuan coast. It was not until 1935 that this country was finally penetrated, by the famous Strickland-Purari patrol.

*   *   *

On 1st January 1935, an exploratory patrol left the outstation of Daru, in the Western Division of Papua, with instructions from Sir Hubert Murray, the Lieutenant-Governor, to explore this last great blank space on the map of Papua.

22

The leader was Jack Hides, a young Assistant Resident Magistrate of the Magisterial Service, who was to find fame and an early grave before his thirty-second birthday. His companion was Patrol Officer Jim O'Malley. Twenty-eight carriers and a detachment of ten members of the Armed Native Constabulary completed the party.

For months the small expedition staged forward their mass of supplies. They were, quite literally, absolutely ignorant of what lay ahead. They had no maps, no indication of the nature of the country, no idea of the population. Papua being the poor country it was, no aeroplane had been engaged for a preliminary aerial survey of the country the patrol was to cover. It is hard today to believe that any major exploratory patrol in the year 1935 could have been sent blind into a new country. Aeroplanes were readily available. Slowly the expedition ascended the Fly and the Strickland, and then the Rentoul and continued across the Great Papuan Plateau. In mid-April it reached a fearsome natural barrier of broken limestone that almost halted the expedition.

Carriers descending the terrible slopes of the Strickland Gorge, here desolate and uninhabited

They broke through the limestone, the last barrier shielding the country of the Huri. Camping late one afternoon on a mountainside, blue robins singing in the trailing bamboos nearby, Hides and O'Malley with a handful of their men walked along the spur on which their camp was established and came to a break in the wall of forest. And there beneath them, totally unexpected, lay the great Tari Basin.

"We looked northwards, and stood spellbound by a scene of wild and lonely splendour," wrote Hides in his official patrol report. ". . . gold and green and reaching as far as the eye could see, lay rolling timbered slopes and grasslands with their cultivated squares. I have never seen anything more beautiful. Beyond all stood the heights of some mighty mountain chain that sparkled in places with the colours of the setting sun. And looking on those green, cultivated squares, of such mathematical exactness, I thought of the wheat fields, or the industrious areas of a colony of Chinamen. Here was a population such as I have sometimes dreamed of finding . . ."

Next morning the ragged, hungry column of this small patrol went down to the country of the Huri. They were amazed at their first sight of the wigmen, with their great mops of flower-decked hair, their light coloured skin and cassowary bone

A typical Huri suspension bridge of cane and vines

daggers. Obviously too, the Huri were amazed—and alarmed —at the unheralded appearance of the patrol. At first the Huri seemed nervously friendly and offered the patrol sweet potato from their abundant gardens; but as Hides and O'Malley made their way across the Basin, towards a pass in the mountain chain, the temper of the people changed. Suddenly, they attacked the patrol. Shots were fired and two Huri lay dead. The starving patrol climbed out of the wigmen's valley, on towards the other river valleys of the Southern Highlands, and to further danger, stress and armed conflict with the peoples they encountered there.

This first violent clash between the wigmen and the vanguard of Western culture probably did not affect the Huri very pro-foundly. Only a relatively small number of them came into direct contact with Hides and O'Malley, and it must be remem-bered that the Huri were dedicated warriors, living daily with the very real threat of attack and death. Also, two years were to pass before another patrol appeared. Life soon settled down into previous familiar patterns, although doubtless the elders talked many times of the coming of the **hunavie**, the white man, as they sat companionably together smoking their bamboo pipes outside their houses at sunset.

In 1936 another Papuan patrol, this time led by Ivan Champion, A.R.M., and Bill Adamson, P.O., ranged through many of the Southern Highlands valleys found by the Strickland-Purari patrol. This Bamu-Purari patrol made the first visit to Lake Kutubu, that majestic, most beautiful of the lakes of the country, but made no contact with the wigmen. In the following year, Claude Champion, and F. W. G. Andersen, P.O., established a base camp at Lake Kutubu, and went on to re-enter the Tari Basin. They walked through as far as the headwaters of the Kikori—called here the Ryan by Hides, and by the Huri, the Tagari. Champion and Andersen made friendly contact with many more of the Huri.

Sir Hubert Murray was eager to bring this last corner of Papua under administrative control. He sent the seasoned field officer, Ivan Champion, to establish a police camp at Lake

25

Sunset over Lake Kutubu, the most beautiful lake in all of Papua New Guinea

Kutubu, to be supplied by seaplane from the coast. Bill Adamson accompanied Champion, and at times they were joined by A. T. Timperley, J. B. C. Bramell and K. C. Atkinson. Until the outbreak of the Second World War, the patrols went out from Kutubu, penetrating most of the corners of the "Grasslands," as the district came to be known. The Kutubu patrols several times visited the Tari Basin and despite isolated incidents, the wigmen accepted them. Their way of life was, however, hardly affected by such brief and sporadic contact.

Had not war come to the Pacific, the Kutubu officers and their detachments of Armed Native Constabulary would undoubtedly have walked to the north of the Tagari River, into the country of the Duna wigmen. As it was, the next contact the Duna had with the white man was once again with an expedition that walked in from the east, from the then Mandated Territory of New Guinea.

26

The longest and most elaborately organized exploratory expedition ever mounted in New Guinea, was the famous Hagen-Sepik patrol of 1938-9. This was led by J. L. Taylor, Assistant District Officer, and John Black, patrol officer. They were charged with the task of exploring the unknown country, 2,600 square kilometres in extent, west of Mount Hagen to the Sepik headwaters, which Charles Karius and Ivan Champion of the Papuan Magisterial Service had been the first to reach, on their North West patrol of 1928.

Travelling with the grain of the country, the patrol entered the Tari Basin. At Hoiyevia, the present site of a station of the Methodist Overseas Mission, it received an airdrop of supplies, something new in exploration in the Highlands. At Hoiyevia, Taylor divided his big patrol. One party, led by Black, proceeded west along the course of the Lagaip, on the southern fall of the Central Range, to Telefomin near the Sepik headwaters. On this long and difficult journey, Black made the first contact with the nomadic Hewa people, hunters and gatherers,

Two Duna men at Lake Kapiagu at sunset

neighbours of the Duna. Meanwhile Taylor established a camp and airstrip at Wabag from where he led his party west, keeping to the south of Black's route. He passed through the country of the Enga and into the territory of the Ipili; these peoples, also wig-wearers, had contacts with the Huri and Duna. Taylor was the first white man to visit Lake Kapiagu, and he made brief but friendly contact with the Kapiagu Duna before crossing the Strickland and moving further west into the unknown.

The Pacific war forced the suspension of exploratory activity in Papua New Guinea. Parts of the country, although not the Highlands, suffered heavily from the war, and the post-war Administration had much rehabilitation work to do before tackling the big task of bringing the country under full control. A formidable task it was. Of the approximate area of 474,900 square kilometres, over 160,580 square kilometres were officially classed as "uncontrolled" at the outbreak of the war. Now, it would be primarily the job of the patrol officer and his police to extend the rule of law to the wild inhabitants of this uncontrolled territory, among whom were counted the Huri and Duna wigmen.

4 The Rule of Law

During the war years the old Lake Kutubu station had been closed because of the shortage of sea planes with which to supply it. In August 1949, it was reopened by S. S. Smith, A.D.O., and D. J. Clancy, P.O. The main task of these men was to complete the detailed exploration of the Grasslands, and to select suitable sites for the construction of airstrips to enable new stations to be established and so extend control. Lake Kutubu was again to be supplied from the coast by flying boat, this time the wartime Catalina, operated by QANTAS. With other junior officers of the then Department of District Services and Native Affairs, Smith and Clancy tackled their task with

Opposite page: A Duna man. He has used his newly-acquired red face paint to good effect. Men normally carry their net bags knotted across the chest in this fashion: women wear them down the back, suspended from the forehead

29

skill and patience. But the story of the development of the present-day network of strips and stations in the Southern Highlands is outside the scope of this study. We need be concerned only with our chosen people, the Huri and Duna.

In May 1951, Ivan Champion, at that time the Director of the Department, instructed Smith to lead a patrol from Lake Kutubu to the Tari Basin, hitherto unvisited by the postwar patrols, and there to establish a government station. Accompanied by Clancy, Patrol Officer R. T. Neville and carriers recruited from Wabag, Smith walked to the Tari Basin, and made friendly contact with the Huri. After a careful search he located a fine strip site at Rumu Rumu, in the centre of a heavy concentration of population. He made a payment of steel and shell to the owners of the land, and work on the airstrip began immediately.

Amazed at this strange activity, the Huri at first forgot their clan animosities. They came in hundreds to watch and discuss the sweating patrol as the considerable task of construction got under way. A considerable task it was: the site selected was over 1,500 metres long and 60 metres wide, cut by no fewer than twenty-eight of the great Huri trenches. Small creeks meandered across the site, and old sweet potato gardens abounded.

Mendi Station and strip, 1955. Headquarters of the Southern Highlands District. Taken from the cockpit of a Norseman monoplane of Gibbes Sepik Airways, a pioneer bush airline that went out of existence in 1958

A fine Huri fight-leader. Note the pierced ear lobe, and the strings of black beads made from the seeds of ground vines

A crowd of Huri men race triumphantly through camp on their way to a *moga* exchange. Several of the men are carrying long poles hung with strings of extra-fine *giri-giri* shell

The only tools available to the patrol were tomahawks, bush-knives, and a few shovels, picks and crowbars. Although the initial aim was to construct as quickly as possible a strip suitable for light aircraft, the ultimate goal was an airstrip long enough and sound enough to take Douglas DC3 freighters. The work, therefore, was thoroughly and painstakingly performed. Soon bands of Huri were helping with the task, although the object of their toil must have been a complete mystery to them. But the **hunavie**, the white man, had steel to offer in exchange for labour: long knives, and tomahawks, and more importantly, shell. These were the small yellowish cowries called **girigiri**, green snail, bailer, and the supreme treasure, the mother-of-pearl shells.

Soon after arriving in the Tari Basin, Smith called up his base on a portable transmitter-receiver and arranged for an airdrop of supplies and equipment. The drop was made by a big Catalina flying-boat of QANTAS. The Huri were profoundly impressed at this further proof of the power of the **hunavie**.

And so they laboured. From time to time small wars broke out among neighbouring clans. The Huri are a fiery, emotional people, extracting the last drop of excitement from any situation, and they fought noisy wars. But Smith and his officers were concerned with one thing only at this early stage: the construction of their airstrip. They worked on, heedless of the sounds of combat.

It is a sound principle, and followed wherever possible by the Administration, never to withdraw once a permanent contact has been established with the people of any "new" area. Unfortunately, the availability of funds necessarily decides the pace of administration, and it costs a considerable amount to keep a large expedition in the field. A severe shortfall of Administration funds now forced the withdrawal of Smith and his party, long before Rumu Rumu strip was completed. To the confusion of the Huri, the patrol ceased work and walked back to Lake Kutubu, leaving stores and equipment at Rumu Rumu in the care of Hedabi, a powerful Huri fight leader who had clear memories of the Kutubu patrols before the war.

32

It was realized that the work so well begun at Rumu Rumu must be finished. With the funds problem overcome, in the following year Assistant District Officer Arthur Carey was given the task of completion. Carey was fortunate in having the services of P.O. Ron Neville, who had been a member of the Smith patrol, and who had developed friendly ties with certain of the Huri leaders. Within months the Rumu Rumu strip construction was again under way. Surprisingly perhaps, Carey found that the supplies left behind by Smith had been well guarded by Hedabi; they were intact.

Again the young Huri men pressed forward to work on the strip in exchange for the steel and shell of the white man. And the normal pattern of clan life was resumed after the excitement over the return of the government had waned. Small-scale conflicts erupted without affecting the progress of the work. When a war of gigantic proportions broke out, involving over twenty clans and thousands of warriors, Carey was forced

A Junkers JU 52 3/m of Gibbes Sepik Airways at Tari. Koroba Station was supplied in the early days by Junkers airdrops from the coast at Madang

33

to intervene. The battle had drawn in so many clans that workers on the airstrip began to abandon their unfamiliar axes and picks for bow and arrow.

Carey, Neville and P.O. Quentin Anthony with twelve rifle-armed constables camped on the disputed ground, arresting four warriors on short order and the following day confronting the warrior groups on the battlefield, to their considerable confusion. As the Huri, perplexed at the attitude of these government men, stood wondering what to do next, Carey ordered the police to fire a volley at a white outcrop of lime-stone some distance away. As the shots echoed flatly across the grasslands thirteen more warriors were arrested. The war was over.

The airstrip developed sufficiently to allow light aircraft operations and a crude station was quickly established. These first buildings were constructed of bamboo, blackpalm and kunai grass. Gradually the Huri clans in the vicinity of the new station (it was called, appropriately, Tari) began to bring some of their disputes to the station for the government officers to settle. Eventually, patrols began to arrest and bring to trial those who still sought to settle their differences in the old way, by force of arms. It was a slow, frustrating process. It was very hard to make free thinking wigmen understand that the government did not take kindly to the old Huri war customs; that women and children could no longer be slaughtered in retaliation for an injury suffered; that innocent individuals could no longer be made to pay with their lives for the acts of their clan.

The Christian Missions were soon on the scene. They were restricted at first in their movements to an area within a one and a half kilometre radius of Tari station. The Methodist Overseas Mission and the Unevangelized Field Mission arrived first, the Methodists building their establishment at Taylor's old drop site of Hoiyevia. Then came the Sacred Heart and Capuchin Roman Catholics and the Seventh Day Adventists. All were initially restricted to the tight station radius, and all were staffed by dedicated men, and women. With missionary zeal they set about the task of teaching Christianity to the Huri.

34

For some years, shell retained its traditional value. As the development of Tari and the Mission stations proceeded, more and more shell of all kinds—but principally **girigiri** and mother-of-pearl went into circulation. Station establishments gradually increased. Sweet potato was purchased in increasing quantities from the people. Houses of sawn timber were cut from the trees in the surrounding forest, erected and paid for. Huri were engaged in increasing numbers to work on the stations and the airstrip. More land was purchased. But as the amount of shell in the basin increased, its value inevitably began to decline. With the introduction of trade stores the Huri began to appreciate the advantages of the white man's money. This was of course, a very gradual process, taking place over a period of years.

Meanwhile, the Duna remained undisturbed in their rough country to the north-west. In the months following the establishment of the station, the Tari officers faced an immense task in bringing the warring Huri groups nearby under some sort of control, and they had no time to spare for exploratory journeys to the west of the Tagari River.

Then one day in July 1953, a band of Huri from beyond the river came into the station, with two gourds of a dark mineral oil to trade. There was at this time a well-developed trade in oil throughout Southern Highlands centring on Lake Kutubu. This was a vegetable oil, reddish brown, obtained from a tree growing abundantly in the deep forest surrounding the lake, known as "tigaso." It was commonly traded in long lengths of bamboo and was much sought after for use as a skin dressing in times of ceremony. Many companies had been searching for mineral oil in Papua since the early years of the century. The oil that the trans-Tagari Huri brought in to Tari station on that July day looked like the real thing.

Oil seepages had been reported from many parts of Papua New Guinea for decades past. Geologists appear convinced that payable mineral oil exists in Papua: certainly, the organized search for oil, which dates back to before the First World War, has seldom ceased and many millions of dollars have been

35

spent, without apparent result up to the year 1953. The Assistant District Officer then at Tari, Bill Murdoch, decided that the oil the Huri band was offering was worth expert analysis, so he handed over two tomahawks, obtained the gourds and sent these across to Port Moresby. He made a hurried patrol west of the river, locating a great many Huri not previously visited by a patrol but not the source of the oil.

In Port Moresby the oil samples were examined by experts of the Australasian Petroleum Company. A decision was made to send an A.P.C. geological survey team, with an Administration escort, to search the country between Lake Kutubu and Tari, and then north-west to the almost unknown Strickland country last visited by the Hagen-Sepik patrol. The planned route would take this necessarily large party through the country of the Duna people. In fact, for many of the Duna, the A.P.C. patrol would be their first real contact with the white man, and with the Government.

5 The Oil Patrol

The country through which the expedition was to move was classed as "uncontrolled." Moreover, much of it was practically unknown. The first essential was a detachment of experienced, reliable members of the Royal Papua and New Guinea Constabulary, to provide the necessary armed protection for the oilmen and their carriers, as they went about their mysterious business. A leader was also necessary. The officer chosen was A.D.O. Des Clancy, the man who as a patrol officer had done so much early work from Lake Kutubu with Smith. Clancy selected thirteen men from the constabulary, each well known to him. He chose well, for the police were to perform with devotion and courage.

The A.P.C. geological team was led by Keith Llewellyn, with John Zehnder and Frank Duke, a field assistant. They were all

Opposite page and below: Bridging a flooded mountain stream, Huri country. This work was invariably performed by the men of the Royal Papua and New Guinea Constabulary, often at considerable personal risk. Bush materials at hand were the only materials used

seasoned men, familiar with the daunting problems of foot
travel in some of the least hospitable country in the world. One
hundred and fifty carriers, many of them Huri, were recruited,
for a specialized expedition of this sort demanded a mass of
baggage and supplies. But even so, airdrops of tinned and
preserved food and trade goods would be required during such
a journey.

A normal Administration patrol operating in uncontrolled
country covered ground fairly fast. If for no other reason, such
a patrol would not risk embarrassing the host of one area by
staying on unduly, and so depleting the subsistence food stocks
of the people. Most patrols planned to trade with the people
they encountered for a good proportion of daily food requirements. The A.P.C. patrol was unusual in many ways. The
prospecting and sample collecting was its prime purpose. There
would have been little value in walking straight through. It
was, therefore, arranged that the geologists would do side trips
of several days' duration, while Clancy stayed with the main
patrol, ready to go to the assistance of the geological parties
should this be necessary.

Patrol on the march, Huri country. Armed police are stationed at intervals along the line, and an officer brings up the rear, with more police, to ensure that there are no stragglers. This is typical high grass country

Moving through typical moss-forest country at a height of over 2,000 metres above sea level. It can be bitterly cold at such heights, even in Papua New Guinea

The difficult part of the journey commenced when the big patrol left Tari, on 20th April 1954. Two renowned Huri fight leaders Piru and Punga, accompanied them. Clancy knew these men well, and with so many young and hot-blooded Huri among his carriers the services of these two leaders would be invaluable. Punga was to accompany many a patrol. He was a natural politician and leader, and many years later stood unsuccessfully for the House of Assembly elections.

A fortnight after leaving Tari, the expedition was north-west of the Tagari and approaching the end of the Huri country. On 3rd May, John Zehnder left the main patrol camped on a flat grassed plateau, and with a few police and carriers commenced to climb a high mountain wall, behind which the Huri had said was a valley, called Lavani, the source of the oil that Murdoch had sent to Port Moresby. Steadily the little party climbed, through scattered garden hamlets at first and then, as they ascended, through moss forest and wild pandanus, until they reached a steep rocky pass, at over 2,440 metres. They descended for 300 metres, to the edge of a wide grassy valley with sheer mountain walls, streaked with white where the limestone skeleton of this elemental land burst through its thin flesh of soil and grass.

Mountain country of the Southern Highlands

A band of armed Lavani men—obviously Huri—cautiously approached Zehnder and his party, and traded sweet potato for cowrie shell; then they drifted away in the dusk, leaving Zehnder and his men to shiver through a cold night. The height of the valley floor is over 2,100 metres and the hard-looking ground actually oozes marsh. Next day Zehnder left Lavani and caught up with the main patrol, now in the valley of the Tumbudu, a river whose source lies in Lavani Valley, piercing the vast mountain wall along some secret subterranean route.

The expedition was now in the country of the Duna. The people were physically very similar in appearance to the Huri, but the Duna were obviously the poor relations. Their shell ornaments were inferior, their wigs untidy and often decorated with dead leaves, bird wings and stripes of marsupial fur rather than the characteristic Huri daisies. They seemed to be more subdued than the mercurial Huri: perhaps a result of the harsher terrain in which they lived. The Duna willingly assisted Clancy's carriers with their loads, and brought in ample quantities of poor sweet potato to trade for red face paint, salt, cowries and small knives.

Right: Lavani Valley ("Shangri-La"). The valley is studded with beautiful little grass-rimmed lakes. The height here is over 2,000 metres above sea level

Below right: The sheer walls of the Strickland Gorge, with the river many hundreds of metres below. Carriers can be seen picking their way through the limestone. Travel in this country was heartbreaking, and very slow for carriers who always walked with bare feet. Papua New Guinea owes a very great debt to the carriers, who alone made the great fieldwork of the past possible

Below: Koi'angi man, Strickland Gorge. His sole decoration is the pig tusk worn through his nasal septum

Phallocrypt-wearers of the deep forest of the Strickland Gorge assist the patrol carriers with their loads. They were thin, timid people, and possessed virtually no shell or decoration, and no steel

The big expedition moved steadily to the north-west, down the valley of the Tumbudu River, to the tiny Lake Kapiagu, discovered by Jim Taylor, and on to the Strickland Gorge, out of the territory of the Duna. They picked their way through the dreadful limestone of the gorge, making brief contact with the timid Koi'iangi, and with a handful of phallocrypt-wearers. These were men from across the Strickland, who wore long curly bean-gourds on their penises, the furthermost representatives of a great culture reaching across into the mountains of West Irian. In June, with the Strickland Gorge behind them and the carriers quite exhausted, the expedition took to canoes to complete the journey down to the Fly River. Tragedy lay ahead. On 22nd June, one of the canoes was caught in a whirlpool and overturned. A police constable and eight of the Huri carriers were drowned. Another Huri died in the mighty Strickland while trying to swim across. Yet another died of dysentery and was buried by the track, far from his garden home in the Tari Basin. The ghosts of the dead Huri, lost and confused, still inhabit that terrible country, the Huri say.

6 Koroba

Late in the month of June 1954, the A.P.C. expedition returned to civilization, and to the most feverish outburst of unrestrained newspaper publicity since the return of Jack Hides' Strickland-Purari patrol in 1935.

The A.P.C. patrol was a great journey, in the tradition of the classical exploratory patrols of the twenties and thirties. The sheer physical achievement of bringing so large a body of men through such country was in itself worthy of acclaim.

Looking back towards the Gap from Tari Government Station. The mountain scene is framed by a grove of the casuarina trees characteristic of the Highlands

No public announcement was ever made on the geological¹ aspects of the journey. The unprecedented excitement of the Press was not directed at the solid achievements of the expedition, but rather at one isolated incident: John Zehnder's walk into the high valley, Lavani.

While the A.P.C. expedition was preparing to face the perils of the Strickland Gorge, an Administration team headed by the then Director of Native Affairs, A. A. Roberts, was conducting a series of very thorough aerial survey flights from Tari. The aim was to locate sites for possible development as airstrips throughout this still unmapped country, and to gain some impression of the distribution of the population.

During one flight, the party located Lavani Valley. This was a dramatically spectacular sight. From the air it appears to be completely isolated by its sheer mountain walls from the country of the Huri and the Duna. In fact the valley is easy to enter, and contains only a few hundred wigmen exactly similar to those living on the outside. But this high valley seized the imagination of the Press. When Roberts told of their flight into Lavani, and of the huge population in the country that the survey flights had traversed, the reaction was immediate. The Director's comments were distorted and magnified; someone used the magic phrase, "Shangri-La" to describe the "lost valley," which, it was stated, contained teeming thousands of a new race never seen by a white man. Then the A.P.C. expedition returned, and Zehnder was found to have actually walked into "Shangri-La."

He was the hero of the hour, subjected to his amazement to the type of personal publicity normally reserved in our society for the pop singer and the sportsman. From all over the world journalists, scientists, filmmakers, and adventurers demanded permission of the Administration to enter Zehnder's valley. Zehnder, a level-headed, dedicated geologist, was amused at all the fuss; not so the Administration. So unrelenting was the international interest in Lavani Valley and the Duna country that the Administration felt constrained to accelerate its rate of development. A patrol was planned to search the land of the

44

Duna for a strip site where a permanent station could be established, and to lay to rest the "Shangri-La" myth. It was my good fortune to be given the responsibility for this task.

＊   ＊   ＊

I have told in some detail the story of the exploration of the Duna and the establishment of the station of Koroba in a previous book.[5] The following brief account deals principally with the people.

Our first task was to examine the country north-west of the Tagari. Clancy and his patrol had moved down the main Duna river valley, the Tumbudu, and had brought back much useful information. The Fox Brothers had published nothing on their travels, and the Hagen-Sepik patrol had cut across the far western tip of the country only. So, although we had quite a lot of information on the Duna country, there was much that we did not know.

Several flights from Tari gave us a good idea of the nature of the country and early in May 1955, in company with Albert Speer, medical assistant, I led a reconnaissance patrol to the north-west. The European Medical Assistants (E.M.A.) of the

5 See Sinclair, J., *Behind the Ranges*, Melbourne University Press, Melbourne, 1966.

Tari Station and Airstrip, as it was in 1957

Department of Public Health were involved in the exploration and "pacification" of much of Papua New Guinea to almost as great a degree as the patrol officers. The on-the-spot medical treatment given by the medical assistants to the bush peoples helped in no small measure to cement friendly relations between the people and the patrols. There were never many of them, and no E.M.A. remains in the Public Service of Papua New Guinea today. Few had much formal training; they were usually first-aid experts and over the years gained such a close knowledge of the people and their ills, that their medical views were usually taken very seriously by qualified medical officers. Papua New Guinea owes much to the European Medical Assistant.

The great Huri fight leader Punga, who had gone with Clancy, was with us. Fifty young Huri, incongruous in grey flannel shirts, khaki laplaps and flower-decked wigs—which they refused to leave behind—struggled with unfamiliar cargo packs, and a dozen armed police spaced themselves along the carrier line for protection. We were fortunate to have with us a Huri interpreter called Elijiah, who knew something of the Duna tongue: an intense, mad-eyed man with a great reputation for violence. Interpretation was always a matter of major difficulty and importance in this sort of work.

Above: Elijiah, the Huri interpreter, standing in marching order in a sweet potato garden, near Lake Kapiagu. His clothes were obtained at Tari. Elijiah was a morose, difficult person with a considerable reputation for violence

Right: A Lavani Valley leader. Note the single large *girigiri* shell set into the handle of his cassowary bone dagger

Opposite page: A Huri of Lavani Valley, with the pass seen faintly behind him. He is somewhat suspicious of the motives of the patrol. His *girigiri* shell is of particularly good quality

On this patrol, which lasted for sixty-six days, we explored the country between the Tagari River and Lake Kapiagu, operating in both the Southern and Western Highlands Districts, searching vainly for a site for an airstrip and a station. We found many places where a strip could be built, but all were remote from concentrations of population. Wherever we went, Bert Speer and his Papuan assistants, Philip Bogembo and Hubert Murray extracted teeth and arrowheads and dressed festering wounds and stinking ulcers, greatly assisting our acceptance by most of the people we encountered.

We visited the high valley of Lavani and spent a few freezing nights encamped on the valley floor at heights of over 2,000 metres. Our tents were of good quality—lightweight japara—but the bitter cold of Lavani cut through them and through the fences of timber and **pitpit** with which we surrounded each tent, as though they did not exist. Fires were limited as firewood in such country is scarce. It is most usually waterlogged, more productive of smoke than heat. It was not until we were on the return leg of the patrol that we found what looked to be a population sufficient to support a station, in a small valley which we came to know as the Naggi. But at this stage we had no intention of building a permanent station in the Naggia; it

was only some twenty-four kilometres north of the Tagari and we hoped eventually to find our station site still further north. We planned to establish a base camp in the valley, from where we could examine the further country at our leisure.

The District Commissioner, R. R. Cole, agreed to our proposals, and early in August we found a suitable place at the head of the Naggia to build our basecamp. It was a small sloping ridge covered with **pitpit** and abandoned sweet potato gardens that was called Koroba by the Naggia people.

In the event, our patrols never did locate a better place for the administrative headquarters of what was then called the Duna Sub-District, and Koroba was gradually developed into the permanent station that it is today. During the years 1955 to late 1958 our patrols went out, pushing into the far corners of the Duna territory, and making contact with people, in most cases friendly contact. It became apparent that Koroba was the logical place for our station and soon we were enlisting the aid of the people to build a motor road over the swamps, mountains and rivers to link up with a similar road being pushed out from Tari.

At first we looked upon these people of the Naggia as being not quite Duna, but also not Huri. It can be appreciated that our initial contact with the Naggia people, although comparatively intensive, was in fact superficial. We had brought in from the Western Highlands our Kaugel River men to give us a workforce in whom we could trust. In these early months while we worked on the erection of a station, using only the materials of the bush that surrounded us, we were forced to maintain an armed guard over the camp at all times. We were forced to watch for signs of treachery. We could not risk allowing our men too great a familiarity with the people, particularly with their women.

Koroba Basecamp at dawn, 1955

This was after all "uncontrolled" territory. The wigmen were known to be warlike, and to have attacked patrols in the past. In fairness to our own people, as well as to the Naggia, we had to work on the assumption that these wigmen could be waiting and watching for some weakness on our part, some mistake, some opportunity to damage us or drive us out of their country. They had not invited us to settle among them. We were interlopers, and we could hardly have blamed them had they wished to see the end of us. And so, as the people thronged Koroba, day after day, insatiably curious, laden with things to exchange for our steel and shell—with sweet potato, sugar cane, taro, bush timber, bushrope, blackpalm—we watched them carefully. We were always prepared for violence, not yet

50

prepared to lower the barriers and accept the wigmen for what we were to find them to be: proud, independent, emotional, infuriating, loveable people. This detachment is not a good basis upon which to build mutual trust, but under the circumstances it was inevitable. By and large, this has been the normal pattern in contact work in New Guinea.

The upshot was, that although we were living on a small ridge in the head of the Naggia, surrounded by thousands of the wigmen who were consumed with curiosity, it was months before we developed real ties of friendship and understanding with them. They were happy to wander our little camp from dawn until dusk. But they, too, must have been suspicious of our motives. It was a long time before the clans surrounding our camp permitted their young women to trade freely with us. Communication was difficult. We worked through interpreters, Huri who had picked up more-or-less intelligible Pidgin or Motu from working at Tari, and who knew something of the dialects of the trans-Tagari people, and the Duna. It was from our interpreters that we gained the impression that the Naggia wigmen were not true Huri. Nor were they Duna: they were

The fine bridge over the Tagari River on the Koroba-Tari Road. This was designed by Fr. Berard Tomasetti, O.F.M. Cap., and constructed by a team of police, carriers and local Huri under the supervision of Patrol Officer Neil Grant. It was a great building feat. The bridge stood for years before it was replaced

the middle people, with some of the characteristics of both. For want of some better label, we called them Huri-Duna.

I know today that we were mistaken. The Naggia people are Huri, but on the outer fringe of that culture and naturally with close ties with their neighbours, the Duna. The true Duna culture is found in the Tumbudu and the Northern Paru. Indeed, we found a strange dislike of the term "Duna" among the Huri. Time and again on our journeys north clansmen would say "We are Huri. Up ahead, they are Duna." The next group would give us the same assurance. I think now that this merely reflected the traditional terror of the land-locked New Guinea clan of the people over the hill. Always the stranger was an enemy to be feared: safety lay in what was familiar. The best thing that these patrols did for the New Guinea peoples was to initiate the process of breaking-down old, ingrained fears of the unknown.

As the rough buildings that comprised our base camp were completed, the interest of the Naggia people in our activities sharpened. Their houses were poor things, low to the ground, cramped, capable of providing only the most rudimentary shelter to a handful of people. The first building that we erected was a store, to safeguard our precious tools and trade goods. It was a fine big building, measuring some nine by ten metres,

Paru men listen to their first radio broadcast from the little TRP-1A portable patrol transceiver. The changing characteristics of wig and decoration from the typical Huri-Duna pattern can be plainly seen. Generally, there is little shell or steel, and a restrained, even dull, use of fur and plumage

built on heavy stumps of bush timber with a floor of split blackpalm, a steep-pitched roof of kunai grass lashed with bushrope to sapling rafters, and walls of plaited **pitpit**. In actual fact, it was nothing but a crudely-built, ugly barn, but to the Naggia it was a revelation, far exceeding anything they could have imagined. They were very quick to pick up the new techniques involved, and were particularly fascinated with our method of weaving large sheets of matting from the beaten stalks of **pitpit**. Our Kaugel River lads were adept at this, and these wigmen avidly watched them. Before long they were manufacturing our requirements themselves; one old man in particular reaped a rich reward in steel axe-heads for his product. Inevitably, their own building methods commenced to change from this time on.

An old meat tin is eagerly seized upon by a Duna man, who will use it to adorn his wig. Sweet potatoes are cooking in the ashes of the fire. In the background stands Corporal Yagi of the Royal Papua and New Guinea Constabulary

53

When we arrived at Koroba, there was little steel in the valley, although a few tomahawks and bushknives were being traded in from Tari. After a time we had no difficulty in engaging as many young Huri as we needed in exchange for steel and mother-of-pearl. A man counted himself well-paid with a tomahawk costing perhaps eight shillings for six weeks' work. This would be plain extortion today, but not in the Naggia Valley in 1955. Each tomahawk had to be flown in from Madang on the coast, to Tari and then carried along the hard road to Koroba. The incredible advance that a steel tomahawk represented over one of stone can only be truly appreciated by one who has witnessed the labour involved in chewing down a tree with an axe of stone. This fact, together with the 112 kilometre walk to Tari and back being the only method of supply—and at the risk of one's neck—are factors to be weighed up in the talk of extortion. In view of the conditions our initial labour payments were fair. At any rate, there were far more people offering labour than we could employ.

Opposite page: Duna man. His fur-trimmed wig is crowned with the breast and spread wings of a mountain parrot and his face is daubed with charcoal and pig grease. The plaited forehead band, edged with tiny tambu shells, carries a small pendant of precious mother-of-pearl. The total effect is harmonious and striking

Huri youth with his much prized tomahawk, earned by a spell of work for the government at Koroba

A certain nervous tension was part of the quality of life among the Naggia. At first we thought these wigmen subdued, even withdrawn. This utterly false impression was quickly shattered. The Huri of the Naggia were perhaps the most vital, mercurial people I have ever known. Every action, every social occasion was invested with drama and excitement. Even so simple and deflating a matter as carrying the clumsy, heavy bundles of our supplies and equipment from one clan boundary to another had to be carried off with a whoop and a swagger. Nearing the boundary, the long line of Huri would suddenly start stamping their feet and chanting. They would race ahead, the weight of the loads forgotten, and with loud cries and superb gestures would hurl the loads to the ground in triumph. Invariably upon receiving their pay—ten **girigiri** shell was fair value for a two-hour cartage—they would charge up and down the track for minutes on end, chanting in unison, filling the air with a sense of abandon. Then all would turn and race away, wigs bobbing, their tanget leaves bouncing above short muscled thighs. These untidy bundles of green tanget leaves were thrust through their cane girdles to provide some scant cover for their jutting buttocks. In time we came to ignore

Far left: Kaugel River carriers thankfully reach the shores of Lake Kapiagu. This picture gives a false impression of size: the lake is barely one and a half kilometres long

Below left: The dawn mists start to lift at Koroba Base-camp, 1955

Below: Puguraba, the Koroba fight leader who gave us permission to establish the Base-camp. His features are very distinctive. Note the puff of black cassowary plumage at the back of his wig

these feverish impromptu dances. The young men often chose the hard flat clay of our parade ground at Koroba for their displays.

Carrying our initial supplies to Koroba from a base we established at the Tagari River was frustrating and time consuming. The Naggia people knew nothing of carrying, and they only submitted to the task because of their passion for the little yellowish **girigiri** shell that we offered them. They would waste their strength in dancing and flourish, and then hurry along, loads askew, hissing under the strain of the hateful work. They simply would not agree to carry for the long hours from the Tagari base to Koroba. Each clan would travel to the limit of its territory and there throw down the loads. Speer and Patrol Officer Tony Trollope, who spent a month on the thankless task of bringing up the supplies from the river, using Huri carriers, whilst I stayed at Koroba with the Kaugel River men building the base camp, were often beside themselves with rage as they strove to keep the long, straggling lines of Huri in some sort of order.

The Naggia people were great talkers. Elders would harangue silent groups of their fellows for hour upon hour. As the months went by we began to gain some understanding of the clan structure of the Naggia; among such excitable people it was not difficult to discern the group leaders, the men of force and character. For these thrust themselves forward upon every occasion. Strangely many of the "big men" had names starting with the letter "P." As war leaders, they were invariably powerful orators. Among the fight leaders, men such as Warago,

Below: Huri bowman. His arrows have *pitpit* cane shafts and heads of blackpalm and bamboo; his short blackpalm bow is bound with thin strips of cane for strength, and the bowstring is of bamboo. He wears the usual bone dagger

Below right: A Duna woman from the Paru-Pai'ela country, pensively watching camp activity. She wears a cap of closely woven fibre netting. *Girigiri* shell forms her decoration

Gabure, Giruwaga, Puguraba, Pijuwe, Piru, Punga were particularly talented in this respect. They derived their authority and influence from their personal qualities only; there was no inherited office in this society. As a matter of policy, we tried to establish friendly ties with the fight leaders. In later years, when we began to appoint Village Constables in each clan group, they were more often than not the men chosen. Many were very successful in the role, although they often exercised their authority in unorthodox ways.

The coming of the Government cut right across the pattern of life of the Naggia people. Normal interaction between the clan groups was suspended during these first months; old enmities were temporarily forgotten as the people strove to acquire our steel and shell in exchange for their labour and produce. But this state of affairs could not last long. These people were warriors, and fighting was their pleasure. And so, inevitably, as the excitement of our coming waned, the clans began to fight.

A man of Lake Kapiagu wearing the "brass" of the Luluai, the government-appointed Village Headman whose role has vanished with the introduction of the system of local government. The beautifully detailed "luluai" and "Tultul" badges were minted by the pre-war Administration of New Guinea, primarily for issue to the newly discovered people of the Central Highlands

The primary duty of any government is surely the protection of the rights of the state, the community and the individual, of property and of life and limb. We understand and applaud this in our Western civilization, but the concept was foreign to societies such as that of the Huri. The Naggia people resented very much the embargo that we eventually placed upon tribal fighting. Time and again Koroba patrols broke up savage, destructive wars, some of them of considerable extent. There was no hiding these violent outbursts; the physical evidence was invariably plain to see. Fire was one of the chief weapons. A disputed district was always ravaged; charred black squares, mute evidence of peaceful hamlets ruthlessly destroyed; banana groves slashed; bellowing pigs, hacked and bleeding, entrails dragging where broad-bladed bamboo arrows cut deep. It took four years of patrolling before we were able to bring large-scale fighting between the groups within a day's walk of the station to an end. Isolated incidents recurred for long after.

It was necessary to open fire with rifles on attacking clans on three occasions. The most recent attack took place in October 1957, in a small valley called Wabafugwa. I was forced to order my police to fire after wigmen in ambush had arrowed several of my patrol carriers and police. One of the attackers was killed. One of our party died in hospital at Koroba after being hit with thirteen arrows. The attack was planned with that blend of skill and ferocity characteristic of these warrior people.

Wabafugwa Camp, after the attack briefly described. Trees and bush have been cut back by the patrol to deny cover to bowmen. Rough shelters of split saplings have been placed around the inner camp area to shelter the defenders from arrows

The damage done to our party would have been far more serious had I not refused to pitch camp on an open patch of grass at the invitation of two cunning members of the attacking clans, while other members were hidden in readiness with bows and arrows in the dense surrounding bush. When the attack came we were taken by surprise. It was an uneasy night for us, ringed about by the Wabafugwa clansmen and their continually bellowed dislike and defiance of us. We managed to cut back the scrub around the perimeter of our camp to deny the bowmen the benefit of close cover. It took much patrolling before we finally brought the situation in the Wabafugwa under our control.

It was partly to divert the energies of the young warriors that we decided, in 1956, to commence in earnest the construction of a road from Koroba to the Tagari. This would link with the road that was inching towards the river from Tari under the supervision of Assistant District Officer Bill Crellin and his patrol officers. Normally, an airstrip would have been our first concern, but at this stage we still hoped to establish our permanent station further to the north. Since Tari had a fine airstrip and was already pushing a road out towards us, it seemed logical to defer the strip and concentrate on a road. Roads have always been a civilizing influence in New Guinea. Roads traverse clan boundaries, thus assisting in breaking down mutual dislike and misunderstanding. Roads engage the physical energies of young men, sublimating their natural

Patrol Officer Neil Grant

Building the Koroba-Tagari Road. The people are employing digging-sticks and a few shovels

Building the Koroba-Tari Road. The people are using their hands, crude digging-sticks and a small number of introduced tools

Below right: Those who have not obeyed the government law prohibiting tribal fighting break rocks in punishment. The patrol camp is in the background

Below: The first motor vehicle on the Koroba-Tagari Road: an "International" 5 ton, 4 wheel drive tipper that was flown in to Tari in a DC3 freighter and there assembled

aggression which would normally have been expended in clan warfare. When completed, government roads were by decree safe for all to travel.

Several officers worked on the Koroba-Tagari road, but it was Patrol Officer Neil Grant who did more than any other person to push it through. A tireless walker, Grant seldom stopped. Only the most basic tools were available for the job; shovels, picks, sledge hammers and crowbars. Our police did not shirk the hard physical labour involved in smashing a road through this rough country. The constabulary in those days built roads, bridges and airstrips as a matter of course. The close daily contact they had with the people on extended patrols and on essential continuing tasks gave the police of those days much prestige among the people. Patrol officers and their police shared the toil and discomfort of long foot-patrols, the danger and isolation of remote postings, and the relationship between officer and policeman was often an extremely close one. As month succeeded month, Grant and his police somehow kept an army of fiery young Huri to their unfamiliar task and they succeeded in building the road. Early in 1958 I drove a truck from Tari to Koroba, to the wild acclaim of the people along the road, who now could understand the reason for their long labours.

The road did succeed in bringing a measure of peace to the Naggia Valley. The people were soon using it, for the first time in their history free to move away from their own clan lands in safety. When we eventually introduced the formal processes of the law into the valley, the road served another purpose: men convicted of simple offences in the Court for Native Matters worked out their sentences on the road, breaking down large rocks into coarse gravel with big sledge-hammers, thus furthering the interests of the community and at the same time serving as the first example of the crime and punishment system that could be expected under government law.

Huri women walk down the newly constructed Koroba road after bringing in food to sell to the station. On the right of the road are pandanus palms

Left: Young Huri recruits prepare to depart Koroba Station on patrol. Despite their acceptance of the role of carrier, each clutches a strung bow and a bundle of arrows. In the immediate foreground is a patrol pack of heavy canvas, made at Koroba, and the most manageable single-man load for long patrols. In the middle foreground are standard Administration issue 2-man patrol boxes made of sheet galvanized iron, slung on long saplings of bush timber

Author (left), Patrol Officer Mal Lang (centre) and Patrol Officer Neil Grant (right) in front of a patrol tent, 1956

Thatching a roof: a Huri man hurls a bundle of grass to the workers on the roof

7 Duna

By the end of 1955 Koroba Base Camp had been completed. It was a crude enough settlement, built entirely of bush materials, but it was comfortable and suitable for our purposes. We had by now come to know well the clans surrounding the camp, and their leaders. We seemed to be accepted. This was before any attempt was made to proscribe tribal fighting. The fight leader

Thatching the roof of the store, the first building to be erected at Koroba Basecamp, in 1955. The entire framework of the building is constructed of bush timber, nailed and lashed together. Small bundles of kunai grass are lashed to the rafters to form a thick, weatherproof roof. To ensure a good job, a steep roof pitch is essential otherwise the roof will leak

Kaugel River carriers weaving strips of beaten *pitpit* cane into large building sheets. Right, middle: local Huri learn the techniques involved

A Duna man of the Tumbudu River Valley. He wears the wings and breast-skin of a mountain parrot across his wig, which is edged with lustrous cuscus fur. A pig tusk adorns his nasal septum. His face is patterned with a mixture of charcoal and pig grease

Author with Duna friend

Right: A bamboo pipe in full blast. Note the method of inserting the little "cigar" of coarse tobacco leaf into the hole provided at the tip of the pipe

Opposite page: An aged woman visits our camp

The patrol on the move at dawn in the high, cold Wage River country—2,600 metres above sea level. Pandanus palms loom out of the lifting dawn mists

Boxing Day, Koroba, 1955. The Kaugel River carriers and the police dance in front of the author's house, watched by the admiring Naggia Valley people

Puguraba, who had given us permission to take up the worn-out land upon which we constructed the base camp, had actually taken up his abode on the station. This close association with the **hunavie** gave him prestige among his people; his manner towards us was proprietorial, and certainly he was useful to us although he was a sour and morose individual. As the news of the coming of the government spread we began to receive visits from curious people from far places yet uncontacted. Our **girigiri** shell, yellow and red face paint and steel axes and knives greatly attracted them, and they would stand silent, watching the work and bustle of the developing station. Strangely, these travellers appeared to pass in complete safety through the lands

of traditional enemies on their visits to us. Many groups of Duna, from the valleys of the Tumbudu and the Paru, came safely to Koroba and returned unmolested. The bush people loved the sound of the police bugle. At the close of each day, on patrol or on the station, came the ceremony of retreat. At the barked orders of the senior member of the detachment the little file of police would fix bayonets and present arms. Slowly the flag of the Commonwealth would be lowered as the police bugler sounded his sad and stirring call. That clear call of the bugle, floating out from a bush camp across the silent forest, is a memory that the patrol officer cannot forget.

That Christmas saw the very first gathering of mutually distrustful clans from the Naggia and from the Tagari River, at Koroba. We decided to risk the possibility of a clash between old enemies. Our aim was to establish Koroba as neutral ground, where all who wished could freely gather under government protection. Thousands of decorated warriors poured on to the station on Boxing Day, fully armed, each clan doing their best to shout down old rivals. The noise was indescribable. Gaining the station, each clan claimed an area of the parade ground for their dancing, and proceeded to bang skin drums, leaping and chanting, oblivious of the rival clans

The ceremony of retreat. The flag goes down to the call of the bugle as the police detachment presents arms

Far left: Another retreat ceremony. The people in newly
contacted country were invariably very impressed at this
simple but moving ceremony

Below far left: The Hedamare
clans storm into Koroba, Boxing Day 1955. All are heavily
armed

Left: A Duna leader; over his
shoulder he carries a newly
acquired steel tomahawk

on all sides who were equally preoccupied. All day long the
clans danced and sang: the men in long, undulating lines,
shining with pig grease and oil, the women respectfully behind
them, shrilling their accompaniment. All day long Trollope,
Speer and I wandered somewhat apprehensively in the
press of the crowd, whilst the police stood guard. But there was
no trouble. The Kaugel River carriers, at first unwilling to take
part, were soon caught up in the excitement. Dressed in a
motley of plumes, shell and cloth, they danced their own
monotonous dance, to the keen interest of the Naggia people.

Then a group of young bachelors stalked into the festivities.
They were gravely silent, decked in close-clipped red wigs with
tufts of soft grey possum fur, bird of paradise breast-shields and

Below left: Duna youth, Paru
River. His wig is basin
shaped, tending towards the
Pai'ela pattern. He is apprehensive of the patrol carriers
as they go about their tasks

Below: A powerful Duna fight
leader intently watches the
activities of the patrol. His
wig is trimmed with cuscus fur
and dead bamboo leaves and,
as befits his position, he wears
a fine crescent of mother-of-
pearl

cassowary plumes. Fine crescents of mother-of-pearl were on their chests, string and cane girdles around their waists, and heavy cane circlets clasped their wrists. In their hands were Pan pipes and their bodies gleamed warmly under application of aromatic tigaso oil. They stood aloof, objects of awed attention for the young women. Some mature men were dancing in the bachelor's wigs of their youth; but not these self-conscious, proud young men.

Patrols now began to explore the valleys adjoining the Naggia, and to the north-west, to the Paru River, Lake Kapiagu and the Strickland Gorge, and to the east, to the Porgera and beyond. Wherever we went the Duna welcomed us warily. We established a base camp and drop site at Kerabo, in the Tumbudu. Norseman aircraft of Gibbes Sepik Airways dropped supplies to us here. The Duna were intensely excited at the accumulation of desirable things that came to us so noisily and

Far left: Constable Pagahau on guard. He is dressed in the famous old uniform of royal blue serge edged with scarlet braid which has now been superseded

Centre left: Two young bachelors visit Koroba dressed in the full finery of their age-group. Their muscular bodies glisten with tigaso tree oil, and their mother-of-pearl chest crescents are particularly fine for these shell-poor people. Plaited cane bands contain their upper arms and the handle of a cassowary-bone dagger can be seen protruding from a cane girdle. Heavy circlets of cane clasp their wrists. The young bachelor on the left holds in one hand his bamboo Pan pipes and in the other his stone adze, or axe

Above left: A Duna man, from Lake Kapiagu. Fine cuscus fur edges his wig and at the back of his neck he wears part of the beak of the hornbill, a bird sometimes found in this part of the Duna

Far left: Boxing Day, Koroba, 1955

Left: A Duna boy

Right: A Duna of Lake Kapiagu; his features are aquiline and he is wearing a head covering of tattered netting rather than a regular wig

Opposite page: A wizened old Paru man binding kunai grass into a bundle with bushrope for use as roof thatching. He wears a fish-tin lid as a chest decoration, and he has managed to acquire a very old steel bushknife

Below: Patrol Officer Lang leads the patrol down a spur near the Strickland Gorge. Note the rearguard of two members of the Royal Papua and New Guinea Constabulary

Opposite page: Paru River Duna; across his wig he wears dried bamboo leaves and his forehead band is of woven, dyed fibre trimmed with tiny tambu shells

A Tumbudu River Duna with a wig brilliantly decorated with fur and plumage. His face is painted and his beard has been rubbed with heavy clay

magically out of the skies. "Cargo-cult" thinking is very common in many parts of Papua New Guinea. Here was surely fertile ground for the germination of cargo-style beliefs. It would have been entirely understandable had such isolated peoples rationalized the amazing arrival of these treasured things in such a way. But in the years I spent in this part of the country no such beliefs were noticeable.

The further north we travelled, the more inhospitable was the country, degenerating towards the Strickland into a waste of swamp, sinkholes and limestone, where isolated Duna families lived in their little hamlets, men apart from the women, planting their sweet potato and taro in the sparse pockets of fertile soil. Coffins were quite common, propped up on pens of saplings in old gardens, silent proof of a considerable mortality rate.

A Duna man. This method of employing parrot wings is typical of the people of the lower Tumbudu River Valley

Fine old Duna patriarch. He carries his stone axe across his shoulder and a motley of feathers and plumes decorates his thin wig

Paru people see their first patrol. The flag flies high in the centre of camp and the people wait patiently as Sergeant Kumbapa prepares to buy their food. A very typical "first contact" scene

A Duna man dressed in a black bachelor's wig. Very few of these black wigs were encountered by our patrols. His face is heavily daubed with a mixture of pig grease and powdered black charcoal

A thin faced Duna man, wearing superb Huri-style yellow everlastings in his wig, trimmed with the cuscus fur characteristic of the Duna people

An old Duna man from the Mogorofugwa Swamp. To bulk out his wig, he has stuffed dried grass and leaves into his net wig covering. His features are almost Asiatic, rather than Melanesian

A Duna man smokes his bamboo pipe inside the men's hut

I remember clearly a certain camp site in this far country. Late one afternoon, after many hours of steady travel, we set up our tents and flies, which were smoke and weather-stained now, in the deep shade of a stand of tall casuarinas. It was the only flat ground in that vicinity, and around us, as the sun went down, were the flickering fires of several Duna hamlets, slowly drowning in the wet mist of a cloud-bank as it rolled across the grim landscape in the light wind. The wind whispered through the casuarina trees around us, setting them talking in the rustling, soothing fashion that is to me the very symbol of the Highlands. It was a night for solitude.

But we had a handful of visitors in camp that wet night, eager to exchange small bags of skinny sweet potato tubers for our salt and face paint. They were poor specimens, lean and scarred, but they were very friendly, glad to shelter for a while from the chill of the night whilst the business of trading went on under the watchful, experienced eye of the sergeant of police. They were very inquisitive about the japara tent under which they were squatting. One old man felt the tent-flap carefully, and muttered something to a fellow. They could not understand, of course. They thought that the japara must be the skin of some animal, but clearly there could be no animal vast enough to provide such a thing as the tent. They stayed with us for many hours, talking occasionally, squatting on their haunches and filling the tent with the choking smoke of their bamboo pipes. We could barely communicate with them, but it was a curiously satisfying contact.

Intelligent Duna youth. His necklet of *girigiri* shell is particularly large and well graded

Old Duna woman in camp. Her fibre skirt is clearly shown. Most of her teeth have been lost over the years

Two shy young Duna girls visit a patrol camp

Duna women of the far Tumbudu in camp carrying net bags of food for trade to the patrol. The woman in centre foreground wears around her neck a crescent crudely cut from the top of a fish tin discarded at one of our camps

At the head of the Tumbudu, the Duna we encountered were hard to distinguish from the Huri, physically speaking. Most wore cassowary quills through the nasal septum, in the Huri fashion; further north, pig tusks were favoured. Many affected the snake-skin headband of the Huri, seldom seen to the north. Bark arm-bands were common; the more isolated Duna wore arm-bands of cane. The most noticeable difference was in the use of the little maroon and yellow daisies to decorate the men's

wigs, the Bachelor's Buttons and everlastings so characteristic of the Huri. Few of these attractive flowers were used by the northern Duna. Instead, great use was made of marsupial fur in a variety of shades, from pure white through silver grey to chestnut, brown and black. Parrot plumage, black and brilliant red, was used extensively, particularly by the Paru River people. At a pinch, the Duna used anything to hand to decorate his wig: bamboo leaves, green foliage, even the paper labels from food tins discarded by our patrols. Empty meat tins were quite acceptable trade items to the Duna; frequently, we found that such litter from our camps preceded us into country we had not previously visited. It is sadly true that the traditional dress and ornament of such primitive people begins to change from the very moment of first contact—and for the worse.

We found the Duna to be a more reserved people than the Huri. Groups of them would stand silently watching us as we travelled through the grasslands and forest, showing no signs of hostility but content to let us pass. They allowed their women

Young Duna from a clan near Koroba. He wears in his wig a small number of the everlastings, characteristic of the Huri. His nasal septum, pierced during the initiation ceremonies, carries a quill from the wing feathers of the black cassowary

Corporal Wi of the Royal Papua and New Guinea Constabulary buys sweet potato from Duna women

A typical patrol camp in the Duna country. The camp is well sited in an old garden with a good view of the surrounding country. The flag of the Commonwealth flies from a makeshift flagpole cut from the bush

to bring in food to our camps, to exchange for red and yellow face paint, salt and cowries. However, once the trading was over, the women would never remain. They would hasten away, tucking leaf bundles of the precious paint and salt into the ubiquitous net bags, as they hurried off through the long grass. Men would gather and watch us as we made rough bridges to cross dangerous flooded streams, but they would seldom assist. They were great smokers, using fat bamboo pipes pierced at the end to take little cigars of coarse, rank tobacco leaves, produced in their own gardens. Groups of them would sit companionably at night outside the men's houses, smoking and talking away, filling the air with thick blue smoke. During the evening rains they would retire into the houses, still smoking.

The author, on patrol, Strickland, 1956

A wigman sees himself in a
mirror for the first time—and
immediately makes adjust-
ments to his nose-stick. It
was common practice with us
to set up a cheap trade mirror
bound `to a sapling for the
amusement of the people

Above: A young Duna dandy. His wig is edged with thick strips of fine marsupial fur. He wears a short plug of pitpit cane through his nasal septum

Opposite page: Once again the corrupting influence of an alien culture is at work. Note the fragment of broken comb suspended from the finely decorated wig. This man is a dandy: he uses tiny pieces of yellow ground vine, seed pods and even a feather-adorned nose-stick to enhance his undeniably striking appearance

Left: Duna man. Already outside influence is affecting his dress—note the folded piece of tin hanging from his wig. His nasal septum carries a fine pig tusk

Above: Duna women in camp. They quickly finish their trading and never linger

Right: Timid woman of the Duna

Opposite page: A stern Duna fight leader. His pig tusk and beautiful crescent of mother-of-pearl are evidence of his standing in his community

Over these years our patrols took us far afield, out of Duna territory and into the lands of their neighbours. Early in 1956 Patrol Officer Malcolm Lang and I led a patrol that made contact with a handful of the strange semi-nomadic Hewa people of the Lagaip-Strickland junction. They lived in the deep forest of this impossible country, in family groups, wandering over a considerable terrain, hunting for marsupials, snakes and lizards. One Hewa dwelling we encountered was nine metres square, set on high pilings in a natural defensive position and heavily constructed of slabbed bush timber. The floor was pierced in several places to permit the Hewa bowmen inside to fight off their enemies.

The Hewa were a completely different people to the Duna. Short in stature, they wore thick cane girdles formed into a small pointed platform below the curve of the belly, with flat cane discs at the elbow. They carried tiny square net bags around their necks and the lobes of their ears were pierced and distended, stuffed with minute bamboo pipes. The sides of their nostrils were pierced and carried tiny quills, crossing over the bridge of the nose.

Opposite page: A young Hewa nomad of the Strickland forest. His pierced nostrils are noteworthy

A communal dwelling of the Hewa people, Strickland. It is perfectly sited for defence on a ridge in a garden clearing. Several families live in this house

Looking south down the Strickland Gorge. In the background,
smoke rises from the tiny
settlements of the Koi'angi
people, several days' walk
from the spot where this
photograph was taken

Hewa visitors in camp; Strick-
land-Lagaip Junction. Their
country was declared under
full administrative control as
recently as 1971. The difficulty of access to their im-
possibly isolated country was
the main reason for this delay
in bringing them under control, rather than any particular
animosity on the part of the
Hewa people themselves

They had no steel implements of any kind, but were obviously skilled gardeners. We purchased from them great pale swelling sweet-potato tubers, each one exceeding seven kilograms in weight, far superior to anything produced by the Huri or Duna. The Hewa were penned into their harsh country by the Lagaip, the Strickland and the Central Range. They had some cautious dealings with the Lake Kapiagu Duna. But the two cultures were very unalike and although geographically close, there was no significant contact between them.

A typical cane bridge spanning a mountain stream. This one is newly completed and the cane retains its light tan colour which will quickly fade with age

93

A phallocrypt wearer of the Strickland. He watches the strange activity of the police and carriers as the thick forest is cleared to make way for the patrol tents. Around his neck he wears a string of long marsupial teeth

More phallocrypt people of the Strickland, watching the carriers erect the tents in an old sweet potato garden. The men wear necklets of pig tusks and cuscus teeth, and the man on the left sports a topknot of cassowary plumage

Pai'ela people trading food for salt. The man at left has acquired a steel tomahawk in exchange for a small pig

Four days' walk to the south we found a number of phallocrypt-wearers, from the Sepik side of the Strickland. They were regarded with tolerant amusement by the Duna as ignorant bushmen. The Duna sniggered when they talked of the long, jaunty gourds worn by these representatives of that far-flung culture. There was once an important trade between the Duna and the phallocrypt people, for much of the stone the Duna used in their working adzes came from across the Strickland Gorge. The Duna feared that terrible gorge country, and the raging Strickland; and our own carriers, knowing the fate of the Huri who were destroyed by the great river during the A.P.C. patrol, were equally terrified.

Pai'ela wigmen in camp. Two are wearing big "bullock-horn" wigs common in the Porgera. Many smoke bamboo pipes. The wig pattern is distinctive and easily distinguished from the wigs of the Huri and Duna people

Two years later I led a patrol into the harsh, tumbled country between the Paru River and the Porgera, in the Western Highlands. We passed out of the far limits of the Duna culture and made friendly contact with another race of wig-wearers, the Pai'ela, people of the Ipili culture who had had little attention from Administration patrols. The men wore bun-shaped wigs, covered with bark and nets of woven string. The women were light-hearted and unafraid, showing none of the timidity and prudishness of the Duna and Huri women.

Far left: Porgera wigman in the "bullock-horn" wig commonly worn in that area. These large wigs were considerably heavier than those worn by the Huri and Duna

Below far left: A young Pai'ela girl. Her beads are made from the seeds of ground vines

Below centre: Pai'ela girls in camp. The girl on the left wears great strings of "Job's Tears," very commonly the mark of the widow in mountain districts of Papua New Guinea

Left: Pai'ela women bring food to camp. They are friendly, but apprehensive. Note the long fibre skirts and body-dressing of clay

Below: A fine type of Pai'ela man in bark-covered wig, wearing a good crescent of mother-of-pearl

Further east we encountered Porgera people, the men sporting great bullock-horn wigs, some of grotesquely exaggerated design. These people, and those of the Wage Valley, had cordial ties with the Huri. There was some intermarriage between them, and the Tari Basin was frequently the refuge of upper Wage people when the bitter frosts of this high, wet country killed off the sweet potato that was their staple food. We seldom camped below 2,400 metres in the Wage.

97

A Porgera man, wearing a huge "bullock-horn" wig. He looks out across the broken, harsh country that is his home

The years passed swiftly; we were constantly on the move, and with every patrol came to know and appreciate more of the qualities of these Huri and Duna wigmen. It struck me as tragic that such vital, intelligent people should be doomed by the hard fact of their impossible geographical isolation to a position of economic insignificance. I left Koroba in January 1959 thinking the future did not hold much for these people.

A Huri leader, from the Paru headwaters. Duna influences can be seen in the wig covering and forehead band

A flooded Duna mountain stream. A sudden deluge of rain in the headwaters can turn normally placid creeks into brown tumultuous torrents in minutes. Huri and Duna people not uncommonly drown in such waters

8 The Wigmen Today

Recently, I attended a function at the Goroka Teachers College, a fine modern institution, beautifully designed and equipped to produce the whole of Papua New Guinea's future secondary school teachers. The importance of this college to the country can hardly be overstated. Self-government will soon be achieved and full independence will not be far behind.

Two Huri men, their wigs beautifully decked with everlastings, feathers and cassowary plumage. Both carry steel tomahawks on roughly hewn, long handles of bush timber. Stone axes were quickly discarded once these people came to appreciate the superiority of steel

The need for educated and professional local people is quite obviously pressing. The college presently has a student enrolment of 400 and within two years will be turning out some 120 secondary teachers annually. Entry standards are high, Form IV being the minimum requirement. Young people come to the college from all of the districts of the country, the majority, understandably, from the coastal and island districts. These have had close contact with the European and his educational facilities for up to ninety years.

Rivalry between the many tribal groups represented at the college is keen, but the experience of living and working together for three years is having a significantly cohesive effect. The students learn mutual tolerance and some understanding of the problems affecting the different districts and tribal groups. This can only assist the solution of the greatest single problem facing Papua New Guinea: the achievement of true national unity.

Some of the brightest and most self-assured students at the college are from the island districts, particularly from Manus, where there has been full compulsory primary education for years past. At the function I mentioned before, I was talking with three young confident girl students, neatly dressed and groomed, one of whom I knew was from Lorengau. I assumed the other two were also from Manus. When I asked them, one girl looked embarrassed and the other giggled.

"Mr Sinclair, I am from Koroba," the first girl said, in excellent English. "My father is Tagabe.[6] He was one of your interpreters when you first came to our country!"

"And my father," said the other, "is Kawagi. He was with you, too. Our fathers often tell us of those days!"

They both giggled.

I think that it was only at this moment that I truly appreciated the speed with which the modern world has caught up with the wigmen. Here were these girls, healthy and intelligent, having passed through primary school and four years of

Opposite page: A Duna man of the Paru River. He is preparing to load his bamboo pipe. This man wears armbands of finely plaited vine

6 In January 1972, Tagabe Paparaija was awarded the Loyal Service Medal (Civil) for his twenty-five years of fine service to the Administration and to his people.

high school and now being trained for one of the most important jobs in the country. Only fifteen years ago their country was almost unexplored, completely uncontrolled, the people untouched.

The first primary school in the Koroba Sub-District was opened in 1957, in a neat little classroom of grass and bamboo staffed by two earnest young Tolai teachers from the far Gazelle, mainly to look after the educational needs of the station children. These people had started in the fierce educational race as recently as a few years ago. Yet here were young Koroba people—even more amazingly in that male-dominated society, young girls—more than holding their own in one of the premier institutions in the land.

Progress in most fields in New Guinea has been so rapid in recent years that one is hard pressed to keep up with it all. The Southern Highlands is still among the least developed of the districts. There is a communications problem to be solved

A Paru River man, his face painted entirely black, pulls at his bamboo pipe

Police and carriers hollow out a canoe in a bamboo thicket by the shores of Lake Kapiagu. The first appearance of this canoe, the first ever seen in this country, upon the waters of the Lake amazed and terrified the Duna people. None would venture out in the canoe, which we built for the sounding of the Lake to test use as a seaplane base

An old Huri patriarch. His beard and hair are quite grey. He has discarded his wig, and will probably seldom bother to wear it again

before much can be achieved in the way of economic development. The problem is being currently examined, although the economic development of the Southern Highlands (Koroba is its most westerly sub-district) has lagged behind other more geographically favoured Highlands districts. But there have been dramatic developments in the fields of local government and politics.

The Koroba Local Government Council was proclaimed in August 1964, only nine years from the date of the establishment of the station. The people virtually skipped the stage of administration by government-appointed village officials, a stage through which almost every district of Papua New Guinea, no matter how advanced today, has passed. Although their council is a poor one, with a limited revenue, it is a vital political and economic training ground. As readers will have noted from the dedication to this book, the Assistant Ministerial Member in the Second House of Assembly for the important Department of Lands, Surveys and Mines, Mr Andrew Wabiria, is from Koroba. He is an intelligent and passionately involved young man.

103

An old Huri man. Age strips away most of the physical differences between the Huri and Duna. Very old men commonly discard the heavy wigs of human hair so characteristic of these societies

The future of the Huri and Duna is squarely in the hands of such young people. They will play a full part in the developing drama of New Guinea's drive towards independence. And although they are very much of today, they are proud of the cultural heritage of their parents who belong in the past and who cannot hope to understand the feelings and motives that spur their children.

The old men still smoke their big bamboo pipes back in the green land of the Huri and the Duna, squatting comfortably outside crude houses in the tradition of their ancestors, in safety now that tribal fighting has ceased. They still wear their wigs of human hair, and almost none understand the new languages, Pidgin and English, spoken by their educated children. The women still toil in the gardens, imprisoned by a stern social system that will not change significantly until the last of the old generation has passed away. They do not understand the new ways. They are content not to know. They still believe that the old deities, including Ne and Korimogolo, govern their destinies, despite the fact that the Christian missions have converted many of the younger people to Christianity. There are elders like them in every part of the Highlands. Their day was yesterday.